Rejoice! Rejoice!

Poems for the Holidays

Linda L. Kruschke

Dawn,

May you always find joy in the Lord!

L. L. Kruschke

2-22-2020

Rejoice, Rejoice published by John 14:6 Publications

© 2015 by Linda L. Kruschke

Cover design © 2015 by Benton R. Kruschke

ISBN-13: 978-1519305503
ISBN-10: 1519305508

Printed by CreateSpace, An Amazon.com Company.
Available from Amazon.com, CreateSpace.com, and other retail
outlets.

For Jesus, my Savior, that all may rejoice in Your glory and majesty

Table of Contents

Pentecost and Beyond

Thanksgiving

Preface

Throughout scripture the people of God are called to rejoice because He is King and Creator of all and because He loves us. One of my favorite verses is Philippians 4:4, which says, "Rejoice in the Lord always. I will say it again: Rejoice!"

This little book of poetry is all about rejoicing in the Lord through the many holidays of the church year. It begins with Advent and preparation for the coming of Christ, at Christmas and in the future. It ends with Thanksgiving and a reminder that God is the source of all we have to be thankful for. In between, you'll find the Lenten season, Holy Week, Pentecost, and more. Some holidays are somber and others are festive, but all are a reason to Rejoice that God is King and Creator of all.

About the Author

Linda L. Kruschke is a wife, mother, sister, daughter, aunt, and friend. All of those relationships benefit from the fact that she is also a follower of Jesus. She is a lawyer by vocation, but her Godly calling is as a poet and inspirational author. This is her second published book of poetry, but she has been blogging for over six years at http://lindakruschke.wordpress.com.

Advent to Epiphany

Silence
A Double Triolet

There is a time for everything under heaven
A time to be silent and a time to speak
As a sheep being sheared is silent, Jesus remained silent
There is a time for everything under heaven

He was oppressed and afflicted, crushed for our iniquity
Yet he did not open his mouth, Jesus gave no answer
There is a time for everything under heaven
A time to be silent and a time to speak

There was silence in heaven for about half an hour
When the Lamb of God opened the seventh seal
As incense and prayers of the saints rose to the Lord
There was silence in heaven for about half an hour

The LORD is in his holy temple; let all the earth be silent
Be silent, for the day of the Sovereign LORD is near
There was silence in heaven for about half an hour
When the Lamb of God opened the seventh seal

Advent

An Acrostic

Anticipation
    Accompanies
        Angelic
            Announcement
Divine
    Directive
        Declares
            Delight
Virtue
    Victoriously
        Vanquishes
            Vileness
Emmanuel
    Expected
        Embrace the
            Excitement
Notice
    Noel
        Narrating
            Nativity
Thankful
    Thoughts of
        Tenderness and
            Truth

Advent Thankfulness
An Acrostic

Angels to the shepherds sing

Divine arrival of our King

Victory now is in sight

Emmanuel comes this holy night

Needs of all mankind are met

Thankful hearts, He paid our debt

- -

Suddenly a great company of the heavenly host appeared with the angel, praising God and saying,

"Glory to God in the highest heaven, and on earth peace to those on whom his favor rests."

Luke 2:13-14 (NIV).

- -

Advent Is

A Googlism

Advent is coming

Advent is a season

> a holy season
> a marvelous season
> a season of preparation
> not a penitential season
> too good a season to waste
> the season that begins the liturgical year
> an especially lovely season and we can
>   make great use of it

Advent is a time

> a time of waiting
> a time of spiritual preparation
> a time of expectation and reflection
> a time of awaiting a God who loves us
> a time to celebrate Light in the midst of
>   darkness
> a time for looking forward to
>   celebrating the birth of Jesus
> a good time for us to live like people
>   who are being redeemed

Advent is

for waiting
active waiting
promise of peace
about preparation
rest for the weary
anticipation and hope
about who holds the future
both a beginning and an end
one of those marvelous little jewels
a period of devout and joyful
expectation
celebrated by Christians all over the
world
a longing and anticipation in the midst
of suffering
celebrated as a time of joy and hope as
we await the coming of the King

Advent is kind of like that

Like a Snowflake

Free Verse

Like a single snowflake floating down
from above so like the others,
but each unique, so the Son of God came
down to earth from heaven above, like us
He came as a tiny baby, like us unique and
one of a kind, but He is a blessed gift of love,
Immanuel, God with us

*All this took place to fulfill what the Lord
had said through the prophet: "The virgin
will conceive and give birth to a son, and
they will call him Immanuel" (which means
"God with us").
Matthew 1:22-23 (NIV).*

God with Us
An Acrostic

Glory of the Holy One, robed in majesty

Omnipresent King of kings, deserving pageantry

Deity incarnate be, because of love for you and me

Willingly He came to earth, left His throne behind

Immanuel, Son of God, seeking to redeem mankind

To leave mankind dead in sin not what He designed

His loving mercy on the cross with grace combined

Understanding His great love is what Christ desires

Sinners to trust in Him alone is all our God requires

Alpha and Omega
Even-Rhymed Quatrain

You are Alpha and Omega
The beginning and the end
Before You there was nothing
There will be only You in the end

You are Alpha and Omega
Your glory will not cease
When all You've created is gone
There will remain Your peace

You are Alpha and Omega
Creator of all that is good
Both the seen and the unseen
In awe before You stood

You are Alpha and Omega
My living God of grace
You offer love and mercy
Never leaving us in disgrace

You are Alpha and Omega
Your name exalted on high
Yet You humbled Yourself
So Your people would never die

You are Alpha and Omega
You promise to make all things new
To take away all sin and death
All that You promise is true

You are Alpha and Omega
You owe nothing, yet intend
To bless Your whole creation
From beginning to the end

- -

He said to me: "It is done. I am the Alpha and the Omega, the Beginning and the End. To the thirsty I will give water without cost from the spring of the water of life. Those who are victorious will inherit all this, and I will be their God and they will be my children."
Revelation 21:6-7 (NIV)

- -

Come, Baby Jesus

Free Verse

I set it up just yesterday
My favorite little nativity
Mary, Joseph, and baby Jesus
surrounded by angels and kings

My mother-in-law made it
She created it the year of my birth
Each ceramic piece of the scene
hand painted, even the angels' wings

I set it up just yesterday
But where could it have gone
It's no longer on the china hutch
where it really does belong

Oh my, I see what has occurred
My favorite little nativity
has come alive in my dining room
It's really quite absurd

I guess I should be more careful
what I pray for as just today
I asked the Lord Jesus
to come into my home to stay

Valuable

Couplet-Rhymed Quatrain

More precious than all the golden rings
of all the princes and earthly kings
the Son of God came down from above
to show us His great and holy love

Nothing else do we really need
when His love we deeply heed
All else He provides when we ask
To share His love is our only task

What is most valuable in this life?
Where do we turn in times of strife?
Not to wealth or gold or shiny things
but the precious love of the King of kings

The Sweet Eve of Christmas Day
Couplet-Rhymed Quatrain

'Tis the sweet eve of Christmas Day
I pray that all will find the way
To the manger where Jesus sleeps
See the treasure His mother keeps

This quiet will last but a little while
For one day Mary will not smile
To see her Son on a cross dying
His disciples all around her crying

But for now she cradles Him in her arms
Protecting the Christ Child from all harms
Seek Him now as the wise men do
He came out of love for me and you

Christmas Eve
An Acrostic

Christ is born in a manger

Hallelujah the angels sing

Raising their voices in praise

Infant Son of God Most High

Shepherds in awe this night

Trumpets sound at His coming

Magi come from the East

Arriving to worship the King

Savior of the world, the Word made flesh

Even now

Voices praise Him

Emmanuel

Joy

Trimeric

Jesus is the greatest gift to all mankind
More magnificent than jewels or gold
More valuable than the newest smartphone
More satisfying than any gift under the tree

More magnificent than jewels or gold
Offered by husbands to wives as a gift
Joy's in the giving when Christ is praised

More valuable than the newest smartphone
Offered by parents to kids as a prize
Joy is in Christ for the child love raised

More satisfying than any gift under the tree
Is the gift Jesus promises to you and me
Joy in salvation, all our sins razed

Epiphany
Rhymed Couplets

The magi travelled from afar
following the bearing of a new star

The Jewish King of kings to see
the One who came for you and me

He could have come for only His people
then there would be nary a steeple

With His cross raised up high
where every seeking heart could spy

The truth is that He loved us all
this Son of God who took the fall

The One whom to all mankind appeared
though by some He was not revered

With the magi let us follow His star
and seek this One who appeared from afar

Mardi Gras to Easter

He Paved the Way

Rhymed Couplets

John the Baptist did not care
What people thought of his wild hair

Repent and be baptized his hue and cry
Messiah is coming, His kingdom is nigh

John the Baptist lost his head
But because of Jesus he is not dead

John paved the way for eternal life
Found in the Son who gave His life

Content with his place in history
John showed the Way for you and me

Jesus increased in wisdom and power
John decreased at the proper hour

Jesus now reigns as King of kings
To our Lord and Savior we sing

John is an honored martyred soul
Under God's altar for his prophetic role

Now we find our identity in Christ
Who gave His life and paid the price

Fat Tuesday
Free Verse

Mardi Gras
We call it Fat Tuesday
It's the day we eat,
drink, and be merry
for tomorrow we shall die
or maybe only diet

We sacrifice the things we love
→chocolate
→sweets
→coffee
→bread
→maybe our favorite TV shows

We attempt by our sacrifice
to understand
the passion of Christ, His suffering,
His sacrifice for us

He really did die,
not just diet

For 40 days we sacrifice
as if we were wandering
in the wilderness, hungry and tired

But each night we sleep in our own
warm, cozy beds
with our stomachs full
even if not with our favorite treats

Can we ever truly understand?
Perhaps not
For today, let's just eat

*Jesus, full of the Holy Spirit, left the Jordan
and was led by the Spirit into the wilderness,
where for forty days he was tempted by the
devil. He ate nothing during those days, and
at the end of them he was hungry.
Luke 4:1-2 (NIV)*

Ash and Sackcloth

Even-Rhymed Quatrain

To repent in ash and sackcloth
Is a concept we scarce understand
To revel in our pleasure and sin
Is a right we fully demand

Yet repent is what God commands us
Deep down we know that we should
Still we cling to our sinful behavior
Thinking obedience will hinder our good

Disobedience displays a lack of trust
That God yearns for our perfect peace
If we repent in ash and sackcloth
Only then will our wretchedness cease

Lent

An Acrostic

Lamb of God, slain for me

Eternal One, Thy love I see

Now and forever, I turn to Thee

Thou are my life — set me free

The next day John saw Jesus coming toward him and said, "Look, the Lamb of God, who takes away the sin of the world!"
John 1:29 (NIV)

Journey of Lent
An Acrostic

Lord of all creation
wandered in the wilderness
40 days of hunger and temptation

Eternal life set aside
for just a time so that it might
be ever available to His beloved

Name above all names
sacrificed for you, for me
His very life to set us forever free

Throne of grace
once again His proper place
where justice and mercy reign

Palm Sunday
An Acrostic

Praise to God the Father

Alleluia to the Son

Lord of all creation

Man He did become

Savior of the human race

Undoing Satan's curse

Ne'er again will evil win

Divine victory in force

Alleluia to the Holy One

Yesterday's prophecy fulfilled

- -

No longer will there be any curse. The throne of God and of the Lamb will be in the city, and his servants will serve him. Revelation 22:3 (NIV)

- -

The Crowd Shouted
A Found Poem

The crowd shouted:
"Hosanna in the highest!
Blessed is He
who comes in the name of the Lord!"

    The Pharisees looked for a way
    to arrest Him,
    but they were afraid of the crowd
    because the people held that
    He was a prophet.

Peter declared,
"Even if I have to die with You,
I will never disown you."
And all the other disciples said the same.

As He taught in the Temple court,
the large crowd listened
to him with delight.

Then Jesus' disciples said, "Now we can see
that you know all things and
that you do not even need us to ask.
This makes us believe that you
came from God."

Now the betrayer
had arranged a signal with the guards:
"The one I kiss is the man; arrest him."
Going at once to Jesus, Judas said,
"Greetings, Rabbi!"
and kissed Him.

Then all the disciples
deserted Him and fled.
Peter denied Him again,
with an oath: "I don't know the man!"

"What shall I do, then,
with Jesus who is called Christ?"
Pilate asked.

The crowd shouted all the louder,
"Crucify him! Crucify him!"

Betrayed, 'Twas a Kiss
A Villanelle

Betrayed, 'twas a kiss, the beginning of the end
Then all the others scattered in the night
Not knowing in three days You would ascend

He was among those You counted as a friend
There was a time his zeal burned so bright
Betrayed, 'twas a kiss, the beginning of the end

Your followers to kneel in prayer You did commend
But they lacked Your wisdom and keen foresight
Not knowing in three days You would ascend

The ill-begotten silver Judas would never spend
Instead his life would become a terrible blight
Betrayed, 'twas a kiss, the beginning of the end

Although his first impulse was to defend
Peter would hide his face from the light
Not knowing in three days You would ascend

Your promises they all failed to comprehend
Though all but one were redeemed in Your sight
Betrayed, 'twas a kiss, the beginning of the end
Not knowing in three days You would ascend

Betrayed and Denied

Free Verse

Betrayed with a kiss
by one whose feet
He washed
but whose heart
remained unclean

Denied three times
by one whose feet
He washed
but who felt remorse
and was restored

May we all be like Peter
and not Judas

Who Is This Jesus?
Rhymed Quatrain

Who is this Jesus?
Some say He's no one
His very existence they do shun
They do not know God's only Son

Who is this Jesus?
Some call Him Christ
The Resurrection and the life
He is the answer to all my strife

Who is this Jesus?
Called King of Jews
The One who brings the Good News
He has become my writing muse

Who is this Jesus?
Prophets say Emmanuel
He came to earth with us to dwell
We're no longer under Satan's spell

Who is this Jesus?
Whose life was cut short
He was condemned by the high court
The truth of His rising some still distort

Who is this Jesus?
Who came as Prince of peace
His love and mercy will never cease
My devotion to Him will ever increase

Who is this Jesus?
My Savior and friend
My innocence He promised to defend
He will stand by me until the end

- -

"But what about you?" he asked. "Who do
you say I am?"
Peter answered, "You are the Messiah."
Mark 8:29 (NIV)

- -

Jerusalem

Free Verse

Jerusalem, Jerusalem
City where my Savior died
I pray you find His peace

Jerusalem, Jerusalem
Ancient city from of old
I pray God's blessing on you

Jerusalem, Jerusalem
A city exiled to Babylon
I pray your safe return

Jerusalem, Jerusalem
The city with many enemies
I pray protection for your people

Jerusalem, Jerusalem
A new city you'll one day be
I pray the Lord's return

The Greatest Winner

Free Verse

The greatest winner in all history
was executed for crimes
He did not commit

He had the positive thinking
of a man of great faith and power
calming storms and healing the sick

He was not responsible
for our great sinfulness
but took responsibility nonetheless

He was driven
by love and by grace
to take the punishment for all

Though He knew everything
since He was God, still
He sweat blood with great anguish

Despite His greatness and majesty
He humbled Himself for our sake
was gentle like a Lamb to the slaughter

Love
Even-Rhymed Quatrain

Your love is patient
each time I fail
For all my sins
You bore the nails

Your love remembers not
the sins of today
but chooses to forgive
and provide a way

Your love is the truth
that provides the light
to guide my life
help me do what is right

Your love protects me
from the evil one
As You hung on the cross
You declared all was done

The Shepherd
A Found Poem – From the Holy Bible

We all, like sheep, have gone astray,
each of us has turned to his own way;
Hear us, O Shepherd of Israel,
You who lead Joseph's descendants
like a flock; You who sit enthroned
between the cherubim.

Like a hunted gazelle, like sheep
without a shepherd,
each will flee to his native land.
Save your people and bless
your inheritance; be their shepherd
and carry them forever.
He had compassion on them,
because they were harassed and helpless,
like sheep without a shepherd.
This is what the Sovereign LORD says:
Woe to the shepherds of Israel
who only take care of themselves!

Should not shepherds take care of the flock?
The LORD is my shepherd,
I shall not be in want.
"I will place shepherds over them
who will tend them, and they will

no longer be afraid or terrified,
nor will any be missing," declares the LORD.

Then I will give you shepherds
after my own heart, who will lead you
with knowledge and understanding.
They will follow my laws
and be careful to keep my decrees.
And David shepherded them
with integrity of heart;
with skillful hands he led them.

For you were like sheep
going astray, but now
you have returned to the Shepherd
and Overseer of your souls.
And when the Chief Shepherd appears,
you will receive the crown of glory
that will never fade away.

For the Lamb at the center
of the throne will be their shepherd;
He will lead them to springs
of living water. And God
will wipe away every tear from their eyes.
So the LORD's people will not
be like sheep without a shepherd.

But you, Bethlehem, in the land of Judah,
out of you will come a ruler
who will be the shepherd of my people Israel.
"I have other sheep that are
not of this sheep pen. I must bring them also.
They too will listen to my voice,
and there shall be one flock and one
shepherd."

He will stand and shepherd
his flock in the strength of the LORD,
in the majesty of the name of the LORD
his God. And they will live securely,
for then his greatness will reach
to the ends of the earth.

"I am the good shepherd
who lays down his life for the sheep."

He tends his flock like a shepherd:
He gathers the lambs in his arms
and carries them close to his heart;
and the LORD has laid on him
the iniquity of us all.

The Last Supper
An Acrostic

The hour was late
His time was near
Emmanuel would be a sacrifice dear

Lamb for the Passover
All the disciples partake
Soon a new covenant
The Savior would make

Setting the table in the
Upper room for the feast
Prepared in advance His last
Passover meal; He broke bread without yeast
E'er you eat the bread and drink the wine
Remember Him, who for you, became least

The Way, the Truth, and the Life
Free Verse

Your way to the cross
Made the Way for us
To return to You
Being forgiven
Redeemed and restored

Your truth on the cross
Showed the Truth of Your love
For all us sinners
Even the thief
Who was promised Paradise

Your life given on the cross
Gave eternal Life to all
When You took it up again
At the resurrection
If only we believe

We come to the Father
Only through You
You are the Way
Your Way is the Truth
Your Truth gives us Life
The Father welcomes all
Who come in Your name

43

The Beauty of the Cross
Free Verse

Were you there when they crucified my Lord?
Did you see the beauty of His wounds?
The mockers could not see the love
Shed in blood and tears

I was not there but in my mind
I see the scene play out with pain
Sadness mixed with the joy of victory
Over sin and darkness within

A crown of thorns more beautiful
Than any crown of gold and jewels
Upon His bleeding brow as
Blood poured down His lovely face

How can there be beauty in such cruelty?
How can there be more than sadness in
The nails that pierced the hands of the Divine?
Beauty lies in the love and mercy beneath it all

The Sound and the Silence

Free Verse

Deafening
Hammer on nails
Pounding pounding pounding
A tear falls

Deafening
Jeers and insults
Taunting taunting taunting
A prayer replies

Deafening
Darkness and earthquake
Trembling trembling trembling
A price is paid

And then silence

Holiness and Love
Free Verse Couplets

Your holiness upon the cross
I can scarcely bear to see

Revealing love of greatest worth
that sets the captives free

Without such love, no holiness
forever could there be

If not for Your great holiness
You would have no love for me

---

*For the message of the cross is foolishness to
those who are perishing, but to us who are
being saved it is the power of God.*
1 Corinthians 1:18 (NIV)

Which Thief?

Free Verse

Two thieves were crucified
beside Jesus one dark day
One thief mocked
One thief believed

Which one would I be?

If I was crucified
right by His side
would I mock and jeer?

Which thief would I be?

If my fate was tied
to His upon a cross
would I trust and believe?

Which thief would I be?

Which thief would you be?
Where would you spend eternity?

Amazing Grace
A Cinquain

Great love
Calvary's tree
blood was shed for you, me
peace, mercy in the midst of pain
Savior

- -

Irony
An Elfje

Rugged
the cross
instrument of death
brought me eternal life
irony

Trust in Jesus
An Acrostic

Truth fell from His lips like honey

Righteousness radiated from His every pore

Unashamed by His robe of humility

Strong and courageous despite the crown He wore

Thorns making His brow bleed, precious blood

I have no other to trust

None other who died on a cross for me

Jesus my beloved redeemer

Emmanuel come to save you and me

Savior of all who will claim Him

Unashamed of His sacrifice on the tree

See? Now He has risen indeed

Red
An Elfje

Red
divine blood
shed with love
offering my soul salvation.
Hallelujah!

- -

The Cross
A Cinquain

The cross
around my neck
Instrument of mercy
The solution to my dismay
My hope

Savior, Then Lord
A Double Sedoka

He died on the cross
Saving the souls of mankind
A free gift of salvation

We accept His gift
But this is not quite enough
For true change He must be Lord

Deeds will not save us
Salvation cannot be earned
All our deeds are filthy rags

Yet true saving grace
Will change us to be like Christ
Feeding the hungry for Him

Why He Came

Free Verse

He healed the sick,
the lame, the leper
But that's not
why He came

He gave the blind sight
and drove out demons
But that's not
why He came

He fed the 5,000
plus women and children
But that's not
why He came

He taught the masses,
and His twelve disciples
But that's not
why He came

He raised the dead,
one four days in the grave
But that's not
why He came

He turned water to wine
He calmed a storm and walked on water
He drove out the money changers
He was baptized by His cousin
He performed many miracles
which John says weren't recorded

But none of these things are
why He came

He was born
for one sole purpose
To die the death I deserve
To die for my sins and yours
To die so we could be forgiven
To die so every lost straying lamb
could be brought back into the fold

He came to die
and rise again

A Beautiful Sacrifice
Free Verse

It is an ugly scene

A naked man with bloody hands and feet
hangs upon an instrument of torture
sharp thorns jammed into his forehead
blood dripping down his face
sweat covering his body

He weeps
not for himself, but for the mockers
spitting at him
taunting and jeering
casting lots for his clothing
knowing not what they do

He cries out in agony yet
intercedes for those who hate him
prays they be forgiven, that we be forgiven
He atones, redeems, sets free
loves in a way we cannot fully comprehend

It is a beautiful scene
It is a beautiful sacrifice of love

It Is Finished
An Elfje

Black
the sky
when He died
redeemed my lost soul.
Atonement.

- -

From noon until three in the afternoon
darkness came over all the land. About three
in the afternoon Jesus cried out in a loud
voice, "Eli, Eli, lema sabachthani?" (which
means "My God, my God, why have you
forsaken me?").
Matthew 27:45-46 (NIV)

- -

Death Destroyed
A Triolet

If Christ is not risen, we have no hope
But the resurrection is our sure truth
Death destroyed wins for us Christ's righteous robe
If Christ is not risen, we have no hope

We would be empty with no way to cope
Would waste all our days to old age from youth
If Christ is not risen, we have no hope
But the resurrection is our sure truth

- -

He is not here; he has risen, just as he said.
Come and see the place where he lay.
Matthew 28:6 (NIV)

- -

The Grace of Jesus
A Triolet

The grace of Jesus my Savior
Flows from His blood on the cross
Bringing me peace and redemption
The grace of my Jesus, my Lord

The source of the world's salvation
The answer to each petition
The grace of Jesus my Savior
Flows from His blood on the cross

- -

This is my blood of the covenant, which is poured out for many for the forgiveness of sins.
Matthew 26:28 (NIV)

- -

Prophecy
An Acrostic

Prophecy foretold His coming

Righteousness He would bestow

On all who called upon His name, their

Punishment He took as His own

Humbly He bowed to the Father's will

Emmanuel, whose blood was spilled

Could not be held by death, He rose

Yahweh saved, His promise fulfilled

- -

The curtain of the temple was torn in two from top to bottom. And when the centurion, who stood there in front of Jesus, saw how he died, he said, "Surely this man was the Son of God!"
Mark 15:38-39 (NIV)

- -

The Veil

Free Verse

A thick, dark veil obscures Your beauty
not the sort a bride wears
that offers a glimpse of what lies beneath

An impenetrable, purple veil
like an enormous Persian rug
hanging from poles of acacia wood and gold

Your beloved desires to see
the beauty behind the veil
and for You to see her and her yearning

Sin, the veil of darkness
separates You from Your beloved
so completely, reconciliation seems impossible

Yet Your love for her
is stronger than the veil of sin
as You died for her, the veil was torn in two

Beauty shone beyond the veil
no longer obscured from view
Your beloved approaches Your throne of beauty

The veil is torn, it is no more

His Scars

Free Verse

Palms of love reveal His scars
where nails pierced His hands
holding Him to the accursed cross

Though in reality it was not the nails
but my sin that held Him there
suffering and thirsty, feeling forsaken

Though in reality it was not my sin
but His love that held Him there
pleading for my sins to be forgiven

Palms with scars reveal His love
where mercy pierced His hands
holding Him to the blessed cross

Risen

An Acrostic

Risen, He's risen, the women cried
they'd seen the empty tomb
with only grave clothes left inside

Immanuel lives, though He died
was laid in a borrowed tomb
as His mother, in sorrow, cried

Supernatural resurrection abide
death defeated in the tomb
sin and Satan's power denied

Even as the grave opened wide
the stone removed from the tomb
as justice and mercy there collide

Now with His people forever to reside
the Holy One has left the empty tomb
reconciled with the Church, His bride

Resurrection
An Acrostic

Risen from the grip of death

Empty tomb testifies to truth

Savior of the broken ones

Undeserving, His banquet guests

Risen is our merciful Lord

Risen is our Holy God

Emmanuel lives again

Creator of all is the Light

To a lost and lonely world

Igniting in the hearts of men

Odes to One who loved us so

Now we all may rise again

Pentecost and Beyond

Whoosh

Free Verse with Onomatopoeia

Whoosh
Did you hear that?
It sounds like the wind
blowing through the trees

The doors and windows
are all closed, locked up tight
Whoosh
It couldn't be the wind
It couldn't blow in

Now we see
Now we know
It is the Holy Spirit
that sounds so strong
Whoosh

Pentecost
An Acrostic

Peter and the others gathered in the house

Enter in the violent wind

Noise like they had never heard

Tongues of fire come to rest on everyone

Enter in the Holy spirit

Common faith connects them now

Over centuries we are connected, too

Sweet Jesus the Savior of us all

Truth resides in our hearts

- -

Suddenly, there was a sound from heaven like the roaring of a mighty windstorm, and it filled the house where they were sitting. Then, what looked like flames or tongues of fire appeared and settled on each of them. Acts 2:2–3 (NLT)

- -

Fruit of the Spirit

An Acrostic

Love —
Open arms upon the cross
Valued me and you
Enough to die for us

Joy —
Overhead the angels sing
Yonder shepherds hail the King

Peace —
Everything is in His hands
All will go according to His plans
Contentment envelopes my very soul
Emmanuel brings peace; I am whole

Patience —
Awaiting an answer
To prayers lifted high
Impatience knocks at the door
Enter not retorts the Spirit
Never ceasing to strengthen
Christ promised the Counselor
Evermore to the end of the age I'll wait

Kindness —
Interceeding for others
Not putting self first
Divine love inspires thoughts of
No one left behind to fall
Everyone treated as equal
Sins forgiven with mercy
Salvation freely shared with all

Goodness —
Oh, how the Spirit does teach
Of all that is wrong and right
Developing character qualities in us
Now, that are God's delight
Even the worst of sinners
Sinners like me and like you
Show goodness from His Spirit anew

Faithfulness —
Almighty God is faithful
I desire to be faithful, too
The key is to call on the Spirit
His power to teach and renew
Filled with His grace and mercy
Under the Law no more
Loving the blessings He outpours
Now my heart remains faithful
Even as my flesh cries, *Rebel!*
Spirit, come fill me full measure
Sweet Savior, it's You I adore

Gentleness —

Each of my words softly spoken

No sharpness of tongue shall I heed

The Spirit in control of my tongue

Lest another's spirit I bleed

Even in meekness is the Spirit's strength

Now for mercy and tenderness I plead

E'er they cease to come to me

Sweetness of soul, overtake all harshness

Savior, by You I am freed

Self-Control —

Escape the trap of the devil

Lying in wait with a snare

Flee his temptations to wander

- (he whispers,)

Cavort with sin if you dare

Out declares the Spirit with power

No lies will be believed here

Triumph over temptation

Remain in the Spirit, stand tall

Outwit the devil by His glory

Love to do good above all

Delight, Grace, Balance
Couplets

I delight in the majesty of the Father
though I cannot fully comprehend

I accept abundant grace from the Son
that I believe does not have an end

I find balance through the Holy Spirit
on whose wisdom I will depend

- -

*Each of the four living creatures had six
wings and was covered with eyes all around,
even under its wings. Day and night they
never stop saying:*
*   "'Holy, holy, holy*
*   is the Lord God Almighty,'*
*   who was, and is, and is to come."*
Revelation 4:8 (NIV)

- -

The Trinity
Free Verse

God, the Father
Creator of all
Divided land and water
Placed the stars, sun,
and heavens above
Formed plants and animals
in perfect balance
Breathed life into Adam
and created Eve his mate
Gave His only Son
to redeem His Creation

God, the Son
Jesus, the Christ
Born of a virgin
in humble surroundings
A teacher, prophet,
and friend of sinners
who needed Him most
Turned water to wine
and gave the blind sight
Willingly gave His life
to redeem His Creation

God, the Holy Spirit
Wonderful Counselor
Promised by the Father
Reminds us of the words
taught by the Son
Source of wisdom, faith,
patience, kindness,
and all good things
Helps us to pray
Draws all people to the Son
to redeem His Creation

- -

But the Advocate, the Holy Spirit, whom the Father will send in my name, will teach you all things and will remind you of everything I have said to you.
John 14:26 (NIV)

- -

Holy, Holy, Holy
Rhymed Quatrains

Holy is my Father
On high He sits and reigns
Loves us as sons and daughters
You and I His domain

Holy is the Son
On the cross was slain
Lamb of God, the Perfect One
You and I to gain

Holy is the Spirit
Our comforter in pain
Leading us from darkness
You and I He sustains

Red, White, and Blue
Three Elfje

Red
blood shed
colonists fought hard
our independence to gain
Freedom

White
pure light
stars shining bright
our freedom to reveal
Liberty

Blue
loyalty true
freedom rings out
our liberty to protect
Independence

The Cost of Freedom
Free Verse

Freedom is never free
It costs the life
of scared young men
who fight to keep it

Reviled by pacifists
who believe evil
will simply pass them by

Freedom is never free
It requires the shedding
of blood, injury and death
because evil never stops
and it desires to
enslave us all

Freedom is never free
It cost the life
of God's own Son
who died to give it

Reviled by the anti-religious
who believe evil
will simply pass them by

Freedom is never free
It required the shedding
of blood on the cross
because the devil never stops
and he desires to
enslave us all

- -

So if the Son sets you free, you are truly free.
John 8:36 (NLT)

- -

Bundle of Rights
Free Verse

In law school property class
we learned about
our bundle of rights

It's not much of a bundle
compared to Jesus' divine
bundle of rights
       — His omniscience
       — His omnipresence
       — His matchless glory
       — His divinity and Kingship

My bundle, your bundle,
is more like a hobo's bindle
tied up, hanging from a pole

We cling to our rights
as if they were our precious,
our most precious possession

Though he was God,
Jesus did not think of equality with God
as something to cling to.
Instead, he gave up his divine privileges[1]

He calls us to give up
our bindle for others
to become as a servant
following His example

And in the process we will discover
faith, hope, and love – and
the greatest of these is love[2]

Not a bad trade, really,
a hobo's bindle
for the greatest love
the world has ever known

[1]Philippians 2:6-7a (NLT)
[2]1 Corinthians 13:13 (NLT)

Man of Conscience
An Acrostic

Man of conscience who
Argued his point in the 95 Theses
Risking life and excommunication
Though fear was abolished by courage
Instilled by God, His Holy Spirit power
No man could make him recant

Lifelong pursuit of his God
Unable to find peace for his soul
Til the Word of God opened his heart
Hope from knowing his need for Christ
Eternal life as a gift from the Lord, not earned
Reform turned revolution leads to truth

Jesus Christ Is Lord

Even-Rhymed Quatrain

Your name is exalted
on my tongue
It will not falter
when it is sung

Your name is Holy
to young and old
It will not fade
as Your story is told

Your name is Jesus
Christ the Lord
You are Messiah
Savior adored

Your name is glorified
by all You bless
and on our knees
Your name we confess

Your Name Is Beautiful
Free Verse

Lamb of God
You came to take away the sin of the world
Simply beautiful

Prince of Peace
You came to leave peace in the hearts
Of those who believe
You are beautiful

Immanuel
You came to be God with us
So we will never be alone
Our life made more beautiful

Son of God
You reigned in heaven
Before coming to earth
You reign there still
Your throne so beautiful

Son of Man
You became one of us
So we would always know
That You understand how we feel
Your compassion is beautiful

Messiah
You were an answer to prophecy
Your story foretold
Israel waited for You to come
Still some didn't believe
But faith in You is beautiful

Wonderful Counselor
Your wisdom You imparted
To the disciples eleven
And Paul, too
Then sent Your Holy Spirit
So we can see You are beautiful

Alpha and Omega
You created in the beginning
Before the world was known
You will be there in the end
Long after all is done
In between it all You are beautiful

Savior
You redeemed the souls of the lost
Were a willing sacrifice for our sins
Your love is so beautiful

Venerate the Lord

An Acrostic

Venerate the Lord our God

Emmanuel on earth did trod

Never losing His divinity

Ever the blessed Trinity

Raised to life, the Holy One

Alleluia, God's only Son

Truth and Life and only Way

Exalt the Lord our God today

- -

The Lord is my strength and my song; he has given me victory. This is my God, and I will praise him— my father's God, and I will exalt him!
Exodus 15:2 (NLT)

- -

Thanksgiving

Thanksgiving
An Acrostic

Turkey, roasting in the oven, golden brown
Hand-mashed potatoes, stuffing, pecan pie
And all the trimmings for the holiday feast
Now the best part is family joined together
Knowing all the blessings of the King
Son of God, who made all things possible
Giving all good gifts to those who love Him
Immanuel, God with us, better than life
Veritable feast awaits, eternal life of joy
Incredible joy and thanksgiving fill hearts
Nevermore to know sorrow and tears
God's blessings, to be thankful eternally

Thankful For

Free Verse

Thankful for the Lamb of God
the spotless Lamb
who gave His life for mine

Thankful for the Spirit of God
the Holy Spirit
who is new life in me

Thankful for our Father God
our Heavenly Father
the author of life divine

Thankful for the Word of God
the truthful Word
that promises life to me

Thankful for my faith in God
the gift of faith
that holds onto His life in mine

Thankful for the grace of God
His amazing grace
that saved my life set free

Thank Offering
A Triolet

A thank offering of praise to our Lord
Rises from the lips of His beloved
I am His beloved, you are His love
A thank offering of praise to our Lord

Holy Spirit soaring high as a dove
Lifted up on praises offered above
A thank offering of praise to our Lord
Rises from the lips of His beloved

- -

*Make thankfulness your sacrifice to God,
and keep the vows you made to the Most
High. Then call on me when you are in
trouble, and I will rescue you, and you will
give me glory.*
Psalm 50:14-15 (NLT)

- -

This Life Is Full of Blessing
Alternating Quatrain

This life is full of blessing
You have offered more
I have a lovely dwelling
And family I adore

This life is full of blessing
Delicious foods to eat
Trees and flowers growing
Their beauty is so sweet

This life is full of blessing
More than I really need
Love and peace abounding
It's time to plant a seed

This life is full of blessing
Enough for me to share
With those who have nothing
To let them know You care

This life is full of blessing
Freedom in Your grace
My soul is ever soaring
I long to see Your face

This life is full of blessing
To You I give my praise
For the gift of life everlasting
I'll savor endless days

Eternal life is the best blessing
To dwell with You on high
With all the saints worshipping
As Your feast draws nigh

The Root of Thanksgiving
Free Verse

Seeing his co-worker get a promotion
Mr. Proud is angry and unhappy
thinking the promotion should be his
Never thankful for the job he has

Seeing his co-worker get a promotion
Mr. Humble rejoices with him
believing his day will come
Always thankful for the job he has

Seeing his neighbor drive a new car
Mr. Proud swears at his old truck
sure he should have a new BMW by now
Never thankful that he doesn't ride the bus

Seeing his neighbor drive a new car
Mr. Humble smiles as he starts his old beater
knowing it will get him to his destination
Always thankful that it is his free and clear

Seeing fat cats on Wall Street and CEOs
rake in the dough, Mr. Proud is indignant
certain their wealth should be spread around
Never thankful for the blessings he has

Seeing fat cats on Wall Street and CEOs
rake in the dough, Mr. Humble is saddened
concerned they don't have the peace of the Lord
Always thankful that money doesn't define him

- -

But he gives us more grace. That is why
Scripture says:
   "God opposes the proud but shows favor to
   the humble."
Submit yourselves, then, to God. Resist the
devil, and he will flee from you.
James 4:6-7 (NIV)

- -

Little Things
Free Verse

I'm thankful for
the little things
I often take for granted

A soft warm bed
to sleep safely at night

The smell of coffee brewing
as I open my eyes each morn

A long hot shower
to start each new day

Music of all varieties
to suit my every mood

Granola and nuts with almond milk
to energize me on my way

Flowers blooming spring to fall
offering beauty to my eyes

Family and friends who help
bear the burdens of life

Access to the Word of God
in multiple translations

A means through prayer
to speak with my sweet Jesus

Freedom to enjoy the life
God has blessed me with

I know that freedom
is not a little thing
but makes these little things
and infinitely more
ever oh so sweet

Grateful

An Acrostic

God created this world for us to enjoy

Rivers flow to wash away strife

Air to breath that gives us life

Trees grow tall, bear fruit to eat

Earth to cultivate vegetables, wheat

Flowers bloom, their beauty we value

Under the sun shining from a sky of blue

Love created it all for His joy

Let the message of Christ dwell among you richly as you teach and admonish one another with all wisdom through psalms, hymns, and songs from the Spirit, singing to God with gratitude in your hearts.
Colossians 3:16 (NIV)

Glad, Gladly, Gladness

An Acrostic

God's
Love
Averts
Death

God's
Love
Answers a
Doubter's
Lofty
Yearning

God's
Love
Always
Deepens
Nearness to
Eternal
Salvation
Selah

Appreciation

An Acrostic

Abba, Father, the source of all good
Prayers of family and friends
Prayers of our Lord in heaven
Ransom paid for you and for me
Eternity with loved ones
Christ on His throne and in my heart
Incarnate Deity, Word made flesh
Atonement for the sins of all
Trinity — Father, Son, Holy Ghost
Indwelling Holy Spirit to comfort
Only Son of God, our Lord
No condemnation for those in Christ

Appreciation for salvation
A gift from the King!

Satisfied
An Acrostic

Salvation is enough for me

Abundant joy a bonus

Treated like a daughter

Invited by the King to be

Safe from the stress and fuss

For He says, "I bought her"

Immanuel is mine, you see

Ever a love I long to discuss

Divine peace I truly prefer